The Thoughts of a Common Man

Poems of Wisdom, Dreams, Reality

George B. Berry

ISBN Number   1-57087-497-2
Library of Congress Catalog   99-75078

Professional Press
PO Box 4371
Chapel Hill, NC 27515-4371

Manufactured in the United States of America
03 02 01   10 9 8 7 6 5 4 3 2

To the Memories of
Mr. A. G. Hudson and Mrs. Jesse Hudson
Mr. Thomas Hudson
Mr. Frederick Berry
Mr. Anthony Berry

Acknowledgments

I'd like to thank God, first of all, for giving me the talent and the words to put this book of poems together. Second, I'd like to thank Andrea who helped coordinate it and my Review Board, friends of mine, who helped review it. I appreciate the support and encouragement of my family, all my children, my mother, my sister and brothers, and my friends. Most of all, I'd like to give all my thanks to the public who support this book. I feel that this book should inspire many people, and that if it helps even one person, it has done its job. This is something over the years I felt had to be done and had to be said. I'm committed to helping the underprivileged and the poor with the proceeds from the sales of this book.

—George B. Berry

Table of Contents

Why

Why have I been a victim
When you don't even know me?

Why do you oppress me,
Take jobs away from me,
Until I can't support myself
Or my family?

Is it because of the color of my skin?
Now that's sick,
Because I'm just as human as you are.
I can love — I can hate.

Why?
Do I remind you of all the evil
That you have done to me?
The jobs you have taken away from me?
The Germans, Koreans, Chinese, and Japanese,
Those same people that you bring over here,
Set them up in business
To keep me out of business.
Those same people you send me to war to fight
Are the same people that I have to work for
In my own country.

Why?
Do I remind you
Of the drugs, the alcohol, and the guns
That you have brought to my neighborhood
To destroy me?

Do I remind you
Of the prisons that you built to house me
Instead of schools
To teach me?

Do I remind you
Of a black man
Murdered
On a traffic violation?

Why?
Hear me, my oppressor.
Listen to me very carefully.
I won't have to ask you WHY again.
The page of your chapter is turning.
Now I know why you hate me so.

I am your conscience.

Two Sides

Do you know
There's two sides
To everything.

So therefore,
To live in a world
With only one side
Can't exist.
To live in a world
And knowing of two sides,
The world continues.

There's love — there's hate.
Without love,
There can be no hate.
Without hate,
There can be no love.

There's happiness — there's sadness.
There's good — there's bad.
There's the underdog — there's the favored.
There's the rich — there's the poor.

Now tell me,
Where are you at this time?
Are you the oppressor?
Or are you the oppressed?

Wherever you are,
How long do you think
This will continue?

When the page turns,
Whoever is on the top
Will go to the bottom,
And the bottom
Will come to the top.

Now where are you?

To Students

I say to you students:
Let no one — not even teachers —
Tell you that you can't succeed.
Never allow it.
As long as you believe
In God above and yourself,
There's no goal in the world
Beyond your reach.

Don't be discouraged.
Grades are just letters and numbers.
Many with A's and B's
Have never succeeded in life,
While some with lower scores
Prevail and achieve dreams
Each and every day.
Your determination — that's what counts.

Don't lose hope.
Neither teacher nor test
Can determine your potential.
You were born gifted.
You have brilliant ideas
To bring forth that the whole world
May use one day.

"Seek and you shall find"
Your own inner knowledge.

Don't accept their label *learning disability*.
It may be the teacher with a *teaching disability*.
The principal with a *communication disability*.
The superintendent with a *leadership disability*.
The school board with a *courage disability*.
You may be trapped in a school system fatally flawed.

Don't be confused by the politics of some teachers.
The ones who embarrass and humiliate you,
Those with no time or patience.
Teachers who say,
"I have the knowledge,
But you have to come through ME to get it,
IF I make you a chosen one."
That shouldn't be.

But do learn the system —
The in's and out's,
The do's and don'ts.
Learn how the system functions,
And you'll be able to walk right through it
On to opportunity
And the chance to design
Your own program.

Participate —
Even if you're not called on.
Learn the basic tools,
Reading, writing, spelling, mathematics, English,
And everything else will fall into place.

Learn respect —
Respect those who respect you,
And ignore those who don't.
But don't let them stand in your way.

I say to you:
Be determined.
Be strong.
Be smart.
Never give up.
Always do what you believe in,
And never turn back
Because you are somebody.

And never forget —
They do not hold the key to your future.

A New Day Is Coming

Wake up, all you people.
Look around you.
A new day is here.

Wake up all you teachers.
It's time to teach a new way.
Maybe the children will listen,
To what you have to say.
They're the ones coming up,
The future is in their hands.
When you teach the children,
Teach them the best you can.
There's a new day here.

Wake up, all you politicians.
The lies that you tell
To get elected in office
Will no longer be.
There's a new day
That has come,
Now you will see.
There will be no judgment
Of color of skin.
There will be no jobs
Withheld from the needy
To give to the greedy.

Let freedom come
To everyone.
The world isn't getting
Any better,
If we let it be.
We got to change it,
If it just takes
You and Me.

I Am Somebody

Why are you staring at me?
Do I look odd?
Do I look funny?
What is it that makes you stare?
I didn't just fall out of the sky —
I was born,
Just like you.

I'm a man —
A man who has feelings,
Who loves, who cares.
Who cries at night
For the oppression I go through
Each and every day.

I like nice things,
Nice houses, clothes, cars,
And a peaceful neighborhood.
Why do you deny me those things?

Why is it
When I walk into a clothing store
That I am followed around
Like I'm coming in to steal something,
Rather than to buy.

And why is it
When I graduate from college
And try to work out of my field
That I'm over qualified.
I thought that having more intelligence
Is better for any job.
Isn't that what we're taught in school —
To explore our intelligence?

And why do you
Put me through so many things
To get a loan to go into business
For myself?
Why is it so hard for me to buy a house,
But so easy to get a loan for a car?

And why is it
That the state unemployment office
Is not doing what it is set up to do —
To give jobs to each and every one
No matter what they can do,
But find some kind of work for them.

A man — a woman
Has the right to work
To survive.
Don't take away programs

That teach us to eat out of your hand
And then close that hand when you feel like it,
Leaving us to starve with no place to turn.

Give me a job.
It doesn't have to pay that much.
I will show you how much I can do
On the job.

Give me the respect
As you want me to give you.
Give me the same rights
As you crave for someone
To give you.

I am somebody.
Treat me as you want to be treated,
And we can get along
Because I am SOMEBODY.

Parents and Their Kids

Parents have been misled
About the way they raise their kids.
I think if you start looking
At the way you raise them,
You too will agree.

Kids were not born
To be slaves
To their parents.
They came into the world
Fully equipped with intelligence.
So Parents,
Don't talk to them
Like they don't have a brain.

Kids are smart.
Give them the opportunity
To use their intelligence.
Talk to them,
And start asking them questions.
Show them you are interested
In their opinions
And their solutions to problems.

Parents cannot force-feed their kids
By pushing ideas into their heads.
Respect the ideas
That may already exist there.
Nurture their inner intelligence
And ask very simply,
"What would you like to be?"

Parents, your job is
To teach your kids the fundamentals,
The values of life,
What's right — what's wrong.
Show them the way,
But let them make their own decisions
And let them think for themselves.

Now just imagine that you had two kids —
One girl — one boy.
One had A's — the other D's and F's.
How would you judge them?
Is the one with A's the better child?
Is the one with D's and F's the bad child?
Think very carefully now,
Because later on down the road,
It may be the child with D's and F's
Who will be taking care of you. . . .

So what I am telling you
Is that society is raising our kids
With bad values.
Punishing our kids by whipping them
Only stores hostility and anger
And leaves an inheritance of abuse
To be handed down to their kids
And on and on and on.
So where does it end?

So I say, Parents,
If we paint a picture
Of the way kids should be,
Then we also must live that way.
Our kids are the reflection of us,
And they do what we also have done.
So why do you get upset and so angry
That you want to punish them
For what you have done in your own past?

Remember, Parents,
Our kids are very different today.
Our kids have no fear.
The big bad wolf, the boogie man, and talks of wars
Were fears from the past
Used to control us by our elders.
When you fear — you can be controlled.

When you are free of fear — you can't be controlled.
But we have failed our kids in a major way
By not teaching them the one true fear —
The fear of God.
This is where we lost ourselves
And our kids.
So old solutions
Cannot solve new problems.

Our new solution is UNDERSTANDING.
If we understand ourselves,
We can understand our kids.
And when that new day comes,
With the help of our Father above,
Parents and their kids will be able
To find every solution
To all their problems.

Behind the Door

What I've seen
Behind the door. . .

My Brothers and Sisters —
Walking the street
Night and day
Wasting precious energy.
Can't sleep — can't eat.
Looking for drugs.

Alcoholics —
Drink after drink
Continue to destroy
Their precious bodies.

Prostitutes —
Walking the street
Selling their bodies for drugs
To feed the habit.

Homeless people —
With a cup in their hand
Begging for money
Or anything they can get.

Sisters and Brothers —
Who look for jobs
Only to find one
That can't pay the basic bills
For survival.

People —
Being removed from the welfare lines.
Knowing that there's not a decent job
Out there for the unskilled
But still being cut off
By the system.

College graduates —
Seeking jobs in their field
Where none exist.
But learning institutions
Continue to teach and graduate
Knowing full well,
There's only a few jobs out there.
How long will we be suckered in
To buying outrageous education
That has no future?

Our tax dollars pay so much
For others around the world
And neglect the needy at home.

All the energy that they use,
Day after day,
Can be put toward hope.
Hope means
The dream you once had
Can still be.

Hoping the drug addict
Wakes up the next day
Free of drugs,
And can fulfill the dream
He lost through the drugs.

Hope that the alcoholic
Wakes up the next day
No longer craving the drink,
But seizing the opportunity
To seek the fulfillment
Of his dream.

Hope that the prostitute
No longer needs to walk the street
To sell her body,
But be able to walk beyond
And be the best that she can be —
Doctor, lawyer, nurse,
Builder of people.

And I say to you,
Homeless people,
You have a choice —
To be homeless — or to fulfill your dream.
Whatever I see in you is all good.
Whatever you want will also be given to you —
Clothes, jobs, housing, and finance.

Behind the door is HOPE.
Dreams do come true.
A new day is just like
Being born again.

You lost that hope,
You lost that dream
By lack of confidence
In yourself and
By listening to negative thoughts
From other people.

I say to you, my Brothers and Sisters,
A new day has come for you,
And the door has opened.
Whatever you want to be,
Whatever you want to do,
Is behind the door of hope.

For each and every day
That you wake up,
It is there —
A new day to fulfill
What you wanted to do at one time.

Take your dreams out of storage.
They are ready to come true.

But first you have to want it.

The Source of Power

We must return
To the source of power
That we lost.

Look to the world around you.
A tree that grows from the ground
Needs rain, but it still needs the sun
As a source of power
To strengthen it and to grow.

A car needs a source of power to run.
No matter how big the engine,
It's not going anywhere
Unless it has gas, electricity,
Some type of fuel and power.

A computer can be programmed
To make it hit everything
Right on the money,
But it still needs a source of power
To function.

No matter how bright the sun shines,
A source of power makes it possible.
Even though the naked eye can see a star

A billion miles away,
The star still needs a source of power
To shine from such a distance.

So where have we lost our source of power
              As a People?

I say to you, Brothers and Sisters,
To achieve the wants and needs you desire,
You must have a source of power.
You must believe in that source of power
And also in yourself.

But let's be mindful of our children first.
If we don't get the source of power
Back into our schools one way or another,
Then the schools will come tumbling down.
We are already on that course,
And new laws are not the answer
For kids who have no fear.
We desperately need to return to
The source of power.

Whatever you want
You shall get by believing
In the source of power,
Beginning with good health —

Mentally and physically —
And all the necessities
To have a happy, comfortable life.

Then I say to you, my Brothers and Sisters,
You watch — mark my words.
Governments and countries
Have failed and crumbled
Without the source of power.

We have buried our source of power.
We no longer mention His name in schools.
We've taken His name out of Christmas
And put Santa Claus first.
We've taken His name out of Easter
And put the Easter Bunny first.
Where does it end?

The source of power has given so much.
He is the Landlord of a beautiful world
And we are the tenants.
We don't own this world.
Does He have to evict every single person
Before we realize that He is all?

Wake up! Wake up!
Soon your dreams will be reality.
The veil will be lifted,
And you will see and receive
All that is good.

The Source of Power is
GOD.
With Him everything stands —
Without Him everything will fall.

News Media on Fire

Yes,
We need to hear news broadcasts.
To know about things in the world,
In our country, our cities and towns.
But we definitely don't need to hear
About these hyped-up, pumped-up killings
Over and over again.

Giving the killers so much exposure.
Giving those murderers, rapists,
Child molesters, school murderers
All this hyped-up media exposure.
We don't need to pump up sick egos
Which are already inflated.
We need to play them down,
Not pump them up.

But the news media
Seems to put them front and center
Making stars out of them.
Murderers —
Like Charles Manson,
The trash bag murders in California,
The Son of Sam, Jeffrey Dahmer —
Murderers made stars

By the media attention
With books and movies.
And now the school killings,
And on and on and on.

Where do we draw the line?
Is this really freedom of speech?
There is such a thing as going too far.
Some roads were not meant to be traveled,
And some bridges were not meant to be crossed,
But the media has gone down every forbidden road
And has crossed every forbidden bridge.

MEDIA — You are on FIRE!
You are burning the brains of our children.
You are making monsters even more horrible
By making monsters into stars and heroes.
Those school kids who go into
Their own schools and shoot people
Don't need any more media attention,
But you give it to them.

Have you no sympathy
For the parents and loved ones?
You create even more problems
When other children copycat and repeat
The crimes that you've shown them
Over and over and over again.

MEDIA — You are on FIRE!
How long do you think this will go on?
You have even agitated wars
And ignored public views.
What about public opinion?
You continue to do what you want
And overplay everything,
Even when public opinion says,
"Stop! No more of this!"

MEDIA — You are on FIRE!
You have burned the minds and souls
Of every loved one
As you show train wrecks,
Plane crashes, bus accidents,
Over and over and over again.
Where does it end?

But when the police commit crimes,
That's a different story.
Let the police know
They are not above the law.
But you keep a low profile on them
When they commit crimes against the public
By shooting people 41 times, 19 times,
And on and on and on.

You have taken races of people and
Continue to separate them from each other
Not always telling the truth,
Just telling one side of the story
Knowing there's two sides
To everything.

You have taken the good leaders
Who have tried to do something for mankind
And attempted to destroy them.
Like our President
Who tried to do for all races.
You tried to destroy him for a mistake
Which only showed he's human.
No one in the world is without sin,
So why do you act like judge, jury, and God?

Then you took a President
Who had done nothing
But for one race of people,
And made him a hero.
He saw only one race of people
And set civil rights back years.
The NAACP was never invited
To the White House
While he slept there.
And for this you made him a hero.

MEDIA — Wake up!
You think that you have
All the power to stay afloat,
But I see a hole in your boat
Bigger than the Titanic's.
If you don't change the way
You broadcast the news,
You are going down, too!

MEDIA — You are on FIRE, burning up!
Sooner or later you'll feel the heat.
Broadcast the news and let it end.
Come back to reality
And change your evil ways.
You are burning yourself up,
And there's not enough water
On the face of God's earth
To save you.

MEDIA — YOU ARE ON FIRE!

The Invisible Enemy

Now I say to you,
Where do you look for your enemy now?

No longer do you have just the ghetto,
The minority people to look to.
To draw a thin line saying,
"That's the Mason Dixon Line —
The line no one's to cross —
The enemy's on the other side."

Going to the projects and ghetto,
Searching for the enemy
To incarcerate.
Walking the streets,
Finding drug addicts to put in jail.
They are the enemy?

Now I say to you,
You have a new enemy.
You have the upper-class school districts,
People that you would never think possible
Shooting and killing.
You have people who work in the post office,
Walk in,
And kill people.

You would never expect they could be an enemy.
Now they are your enemies.

I say to you,
The worst is yet to come.
You will find, sooner than you think,
Policemen among you,
Walking into police stations,
Shooting up police.
Congressmen walking into government buildings,
Shooting each other.
People walking into hospitals,
Shooting each other.
Firemen turning against each other.
All the places that you have held sacred,
Will explode in your face.

Now, where do you find the enemy to fight?
The enemy to incarcerate?
Now the enemy is among you — INVISIBLE.

How can you fight one you cannot see?
How can you fight yourself?

Coming Together As One

My Brothers and Sisters,
We must come back together
As it was long, long ago.
We have to stop blaming each other
For the reasons that we don't stick together.
If each and every one of us
Would help just one person,
All that would change.

We have to become a family,
One family again,
Being able to share ideas,
Educating ourselves in different areas,
And coming back and teaching the ones
Who can't afford to educate themselves.

If you were a plumber,
Then take someone under your wing,
And teach him to be a plumber.
If you were a carpenter, a housebuilder, a bricklayer,
A computer programmer or technician — whatever it may be —
Help someone who couldn't afford the schooling,
And share all your skills, trades, and knowledge
With your Brothers and Sisters.
This will strengthen our relationship with each other
And enrich all our lives.

For those who are wealthy
Or have enough to go around,
Reach back and pull someone else forward.
Share your ideas and experiences
So that they may also benefit and succeed.

If you see children — not your own children —
Look out for them as you would want someone
To look out after yours — coming together as one.
If you have food, clothes, shelter —
Whatever it is you can share —
Remember that something is better than nothing.

For those who can afford to go to college,
Come back and share your knowledge.
Teach and guide as many people as you can.
Then we will build a bond so strong,
Nothing in the world
Will be able to tear us apart.

We have already been through
Trials and tribulations with each other,
And we have survived.
There is a reason for our survival.
We have to take all the negatives,
Erase and replace them
With all the positives.

Never have doubt
Because this you can do.

Let us be a source of strength for each other.
Let us be the eyes and ears for each other.
Let us be the hands that reach out to each other
And come strongly together as one.
Let us not continue to talk about each other
Unless we can say something good.
You'll never have to whisper
As long as you voice kind thoughts.

Let us forgive our Sisters and Brothers and forget.
Let us come to each other's rescue
And do everything possible to work together.
When you greet your Sisters and Brothers,
Embrace them with outstretched arms and a hug,
And let the conversation end with, *"I love you."*

Now we are one.

Justice Overruled

Yes, trying to get equal justice
Is just like trying to find
A needle in a haystack — except —
You'd have better luck in the haystack.

Just what are these courts made of?
If we are all created equal,
Why should we all rise
For the judge's entrance?
Is he supposed to be a god?
All men were created equal in God's eyes,
So why would one be better than the other?

And why are lawyers able to pick certain judges
To go in front of if judges are really fair?
Then lawyers cooperate with the DA and courts
Charging the client a totally outrageous fee
To strike a plea bargain and lower the sentence.
But meanwhile they drain the client of all his money.
These lawyers put their own gain above the client.
What kind of justice is that?

Why is it when the police
Commit a crime against a black person,
It's always a low profile approach,
And the sentence is never as severe
As when the public commits a crime against them?
The police are not above the law,
And as public servants supposedly upholding the law,
They should pay even more dearly for breaking the law
When they are supposed to represent it.

We've been slapped in the face
With cops shooting innocent people
And tampering with evidence.
Some police officers arrest black people
And intentionally aggravate them for an excuse
To charge them with more disorderly crimes.
We have monsters in uniform in the police department
With the infiltration of the Ku Klux Klan there.
So now monsters wear police uniforms
Complete with badge, gun, and license
To kill at will and get away with it.

You know that the court system is very unfair
When you see two different laws —
One for the rich — one for the poor.
More Blacks are killed by police violence
Than Blacks shooting themselves,

Being run over by a car,
Or just dying naturally.
A recent survey showed 85% of Whites
And 15% of Blacks and Hispanics on drugs.
Yet 95% of people arrested for drugs are Blacks.
Now that should tell you something about the court system.

So where does it end?
It begins in our courts
And it must end in our courts.
Every time you walk into courtrooms,
It seems like justice is overruled.
We can't buy justice,
No matter how much money we spend.
Seems like of every ten
Who go into the courtroom,
Nine go to jail and one goes free.
Again justice is overruled.

If a man goes to jail and serves his time,
He should come out with a clean record
To function in society, get a job,
And support himself or his family.
Instead he's a marked man
With a record exposed to anybody.

Jail is for murderers, rapists,
Child molesters, people guilty of espionage,
The top dope dealers who smuggle billions
And billions of dollars of dope into this country.
All the rest should be set free, pay a fine,
Given job training and a job to prove themselves.
But instead of justice reigning,
The almighty dollar rules.

If these are the United States
With all states united,
Why does the same crime
Committed in two different states
Have two different sentences?
How can that be equal justice
In these United States?

If the crime is the same,
The sentence should be the same,
Regardless of the state.
One state should not have advantage over another,
Just as one race should not have advantage over another.

So, how do we take care of this problem?
We must protest the courts.
We must protest Congress.
We must protest the Justice Department

To let them know they are not fooling us —
Not one bit.
As long as it takes to change things,
We should be there.
Those judges who ruled against us
Will be reversed and ruled against themselves.
We must protest until the end of time,
If it takes that long.

Let us lay ourselves down
And be the rock that our Brothers and Sisters
Can step across to find justice.
Then no longer will anyone have to face
    JUSTICE OVERRULED.

Another Slap in the Face

You know,
We go through each and every day
Trying to do and be the best we can
In our homes, in our communities,
And especially on our jobs.
We try so very hard for promotions,
And when they come along,
I sometimes wonder
If this is a promotion,
Or is it really a slap in the face.

Why is it every time a black man
Gets a promotion, the work load gets heavier
Than for his white counterpart
Who held the same position?
Six new duties are added on,
Tripling his work load
And eliminating jobs other men depended on.
The black man trains and helps
So many people on the job,
Yet when the time comes for his promotion,
He's told he needs more training.

All that he does on the job
To help in every way
Is not appreciated.
Another slap in the face.

In this society a black man
Has to be ten times better
And have a college degree
For the same job a white man gets
With a high school education.
Another slap in the face.

Sometimes I wonder why life is so hard,
So much stress, pain, and aggravation
Put upon our shoulders.
I know why —
This is basic training
For good things to come.
We struggle each and every day
On our jobs, in school, in the grocery store,
The shoe store, the clothing store,
And still get no respect.
Always a joke.
When will they take us seriously?

What is holding us back?
We have so much to offer,
And so little to gain within this system.
We have new ideas ready to explode
And become reality.
But no one wants to hear them —
No one wants to accept them.
We can make small businesses into corporations —
And small corporations into giants.
But it seems like they have a leash on us
And won't let us go any further than two steps.
Another slap in the face.

Night after night I lay myself down to sleep
Wondering why and when these chains
Will be taken from my hands and feet.
I want to strive —
I want to give all I can
To make this country a better place
For my Brothers and Sisters.
But I see so much that makes me cry.
Each and every night
I wipe the tears from my eyes,
Knowing I have to be a stronger man
To face my oppressor again.

Oh, my Lord,
Release me from these chains
So I can become the man You want me to be
And I'll never have to worry
About another slap in the face again.

Riches, Fortune, and Fame

The price of riches, fortune, and fame is sadness.
Some people work all their lives
To get everything they ever wanted.
They have no wants or worries in life,
But find themselves stuck in the hole they've dug.
They've become so rich and so famous
That they can't handle it,
And it fizzles out
Just like an Alka Seltzer.

Having everything you want
Removes the most important things you have —
Happiness and your health.
You have all you need
If you just look inside
And be satisfied with yourself,
And having just enough.
That will bring more happiness to you
Than having more than enough.

You become so rich,
You can't tell who your friends are.
You have to pay dearly for everything you get.
Oh, people will do favors for you,
But there's always a price.

How many people can you trust,
And where are your real friends?

Some people work themselves for materialistic gain
By sacrificing their bodies,
Not recognizing the most important thing
Within themselves is their health.
Once your health is gone,
All the money in the world
Can never bring it back.
To sacrifice your health for wealth
Is an everlasting sadness
For the ones who want more
Than they need.

What's important to you,
And what makes you happy?
Success is having just enough,
Having true friends and a supporting family,
And sharing whatever you have.

Look at the rich.
They're defensive, worried,
Suspicious, and empty,
Preoccupied with counting
And hoarding their money.

Then look at the poor.
Their faces shine from within,
With laughter that rings deep and warm.
Their arms are open to embrace,
And their hearts are free to give.
Which of the two seems truly happy?

Check yourself.
How many cars can you drive,
How many rooms can you sleep in,
How many pairs of shoes can you wear,
And how much money can you spend
At one time?

Rich is having a God that you love and fear,
Peace of mind, good health, and satisfaction.
Rich is having a job that will pay your bills,
Being around ordinary, decent people,
And having a blessed family.
Rich is loving yourself and what you stand for.

You weigh the evidence.
Your health and happiness are too precious
To gamble with for riches, fortune, and fame,
Which will only bring you sadness.

I Am Your Friend

Call me whenever you need me,
Whenever you're in trouble.
I'll be your bridge over troubled waters.
When you need someone to talk to,
Or you're feeling down,
Call me — I'll be there
To uplift you and comfort you.

If you have problems financially,
Call me — I'll be there for you.
We'll work it out together,
Because I am your friend.

Sometimes you won't see me,
But when you need me,
I will always be there.
I will never let you down.
I am your mountain lion,
Watching over you.
I will protect you
In any way I possibly can.
I am there for you,
Because I am your friend.

If it takes trains, boats, planes, cars,
Whatever it takes to get there
When you need me.
I will walk if I have to,
Because I am your friend.

If you have family problems,
And need someone to talk to and
Help sort out your problems,
Just call me.
I will be there.

Never wait until you feel that
You need help in such a bad way.
Whatever it is, no matter what it is,
I will be there.

At night when you can't sleep,
Pick up the phone and call me.
We'll talk it through,
Until you close your eyes,
And I can hear you breathing, sleeping,
Over the phone,
Because I will be there for you.

When you're down and out — I will bring you back.
If you should fall — I will pick you up.
If you grow weak — I will make you strong.
If you are sick — I will be there until you become well,
Because I am your friend.

All My Children and Me

I find myself very weary over my children.
Looking at some of the things I scold them for
And looking over my own life,
I find that I did the same things.

Hollering, screaming at them for things I have done.
Telling them how education is very important.
To learn, even though you feel you don't want to,
Always learn something you're involved in — like the system.
Learn your way home, how to go to the store, how to cook,
How to clean, learn how to dress yourself.
These things you need to do in life,
So get educated, learn the system.
Learn how to function in it,
Not how to be caught up in it.
That is education.

As I look at my children,
I see myself,
Knowing that my children are me.
The do's and don'ts I was told and ignored,
My children follow suit.
They're going down the same path I traveled,
And I ask why they don't listen —
My advice is to their benefit.

But neither did I listen when my mother
Told me certain things, going down the trail
She warned me against.
Doing things she told me not to do.

How can I stop them from
Traveling the same road I did?
I had to change my course.
If I continued to do wrong,
They would do wrong.

So I prayed, asking God to teach me
How to be a better person.
How to teach my kids.
And He did.

I awoke one morning,
Finding myself altogether different.
I started watching my children,
Noticing the things that they did,
And I started to reminisce,
My mind going back remembering that
I did the same as them at one time.

So I changed the way I lived.
I started doing good things,
Taking them off the course of bad,

So that when they came to the end
Of the road of the bad,
They could go to the next road —
The road of good which I did.

Changing myself will change them,
Because all of my children are in me.
I will do all I can to see them through
The cloudy days of my bad,
Which they inherited.

I dedicate the rest of my life to them
To see that they have all the rich inheritance
Of good that I can offer
By showing them the right way.
Changing myself will change them.

Any kind of correction you want to give your kids,
Correct yourself first, and they will change their course,
Because all of your children are in you.
If you sow bad — they will do bad.
If you sow good — they will do good.
Watch, look, listen, and you will see.
You cannot preach unless you practice what you preach.

I will live the rest of my life out
Trying to do good, so that the course
Of their lives will change.
Because of me, they have strayed
From the road of good.

I need to bring them back
To the road of good.
I owe them that much —
To change their course so they may have
A brighter, better future.
Because all of my children are in me.

When the Storm Comes

When the storm comes
There will be no place
For you to hide.
You have hidden yourself
As much as you can.

You won't have to go
To the grocery stores
And pick the shelves clean,
Because you won't know
When the storm comes.

The news broadcasters
Will not be able to detect
Any signs or warn you.
You will have to clean up
Your act, starting today.
Time is wasting.

You have done so much bad.
Now it's time for you —
And you only —
To repent for what you have done.

You have taken a nation of people
And nearly made them extinct.
You have put them on a small
Piece of land and called it
Their reservation.
You have taken everything
That they owned.
You've even taken their pride,
Self-respect, and dignity,
And you still have control over them.
Where will it end?

You have brought people over here on boats,
Chained side by side,
With them sleeping in their waste,
And enslaved them.
You've never apologized to either one.
Where will it end?

You have taken jobs.
You've taken our social security numbers
And marked them to tell blacks from whites.
Where will it end?

You've taken our court system,
Corrupted it
Making innocent people spend money

That they couldn't afford
To hire lawyers,
Just to feed into the system.
All money should have been returned
When they were proven innocent.
You throw the book on small charges,
When a slap on the hand
And a stiff warning would have been enough.
But instead you had to try
To make a name for yourself.
Where will it end?

You have stockpiled guns and food
For something you don't even know,
Trying to prepare yourself
For the new century.
You've taken money out of the bank,
But what good will it be
When there will be nothing to buy
When the storm comes.

You won't know when the storm comes.
You won't be prepared —
You won't be able to stockpile anything
When the storm comes.

I say to you, my Brother,
Apologize.
Admit your guilt.
Give back everything
That you have taken.
Or all will be taken from you,
When the storm comes.
And you won't know.

Trading Places

Oh, I've seen so many things
In my life that hurt me so bad.
I sit back and reminisce
All the hurt and pain that I've seen.
I wish that it will never go away,
Because it makes me wiser —
It makes me stronger.

Things that I remember
Bring so much pain
That I can't bear it.
The time when the church
Was bombed and three little,
Innocent girls in church worshipping
Their God were killed —
Killed by some clowns wearing
Dummy hats and white sheets.

I remember the aggravation
From the protesting.
People just wanted
To have equal rights,
To have a voice,
To have good jobs,
To be able to go to restaurants,

To bathrooms.
But they got dogs sicced on them,
Water hoses sprayed on them,
Just walking the street
In a mild manner, protesting,
To have all this madness
Afflicted upon them.

Oh, yes,
I remember the lynching of my Brother,
Just walking through the woods whistling
And people came, took him away,
Said he was whistling at a lady
Of another color,
And hung him.
So much pain,
But I do remember.

I remember a man
Being strapped
To the back of a truck
And dragged for miles,
Disfiguring him,
Dismembering his limbs and head.

I will never ever trade places
With that kind of anger

Of my oppressor.
On the job he oppressed me
By giving me more money,
But not the promotion or respect.
He thought the money could buy me.
Putting me in charge of people
Who didn't even want to listen,
Because I was of a different race.
I worked so hard to do my best
By educating myself,
To climb as high as I could,
Yet the ladder of opportunity
Had very few steps on it
For me to climb.
So I wonder,
Why did I give so much love out,
And get so much hatred back.

Oh, yes,
I remember the pain,
But I would give nothing to change
Who I am and what I am.
If we ever trade places
To have our day and time,
I will never be what they are.
I will always think of
Forgiving and loving —

Never have the hate
That they had for me.

I would never trade places for that,
Because I know that in time,
Bad and evil don't last forever.
Love always comes to the top.
Love always wins.
There are times that I feel
Nothing is going right,
But I will never trade places
With my oppressor.

Where does the anger come from?
Why do people have to be so mad
To do another one the way they do?
What makes a person build up
So much hatred and anger,
To step on, to walk on, to spit on
Another human being
And treat this human being
As though he were less than human.

What makes a person like that
Live on this beautiful earth,
That has so much to give,
And he takes so much away.

How long does he think this will last?
When the page turns
And I take my place on top,
I will never, ever afflict oppression
Upon them as they did me.
I will never trade places with them.
If they hate me —
I'll love them.

I will always tell my Brothers and Sisters,
"Look over the ignorant.
People who have so much hatred
In their hearts,
Can't have one."

I remember the day
When we spoke of the Motherland,
Hating our Brothers and Sisters
Who helped send us here.
I say to you now,
The hate must stop
Because they're suffering
Right along with us.
They're paying their debt
For what they've done.

So I say,
Forgive and forget.
Never be like your oppressor.
Reach out with love and forgiveness
In your heart.
And never trade places with him.

The Shrinking Race

You know, going back long ago,
There was just one, and one brought many.
And as it expanded, the human race fell
Like leaves from a tree,
Scattered all over the world
As many different races.

But no one race should have
Control over all races.
That evil is why you are shrinking.
And now the races will come back to one.
No longer will you have the power
To control the whole human race,
Because you are shrinking,
And you do know this.

Now you're doing everything
In your power to stop what's to happen,
But you cannot stop it.
The more you try,
The quicker you shrink.

You cannot stop the interracial breeding
Because a race with no color
Cannot stand forever.

It has to go back to where it came,
And that's from color.

You've tried to use the fertility drug
To create more babies to multiply your race.
But you've forgotten one fact —
The thinner you spread things,
The weaker they are.
The intelligence won't be there —
The immune system won't be there.
The only thing you're creating
Is a very weak race of people.

Now you've come up with the idea of cloning,
And eventually you'll be cloning human beings
As you have done animals.
You will try to find the most intelligent people
To clone to try to make your race stronger and smarter.
But that won't work because there is a very thin line
Between a genius and a nut.

You have tried to stop our population
By the unknown that is happening
To black babies in hospitals.

The mortality rate of suspicious deaths
In our hospitals among black kids has gone up.

You have incarcerated our young black men,
Not for very vicious crimes, but for small crimes,
And gave them a lot of time to keep them behind bars,
To rob them of their youthful, child-producing years.

You have sent our black men into war,
And you have put them on the front line
To narrow the black population of men.

You have created birth control
And put it among our black women
To slow down the black population.
You have brought contraceptives
That you have scared people into using
To stop the race population.

But you find out that none of that is working
Because the race will grow stronger
As you try to eliminate it.
It will become stronger
And you will become weaker.
So it is time for you to face reality
And accept what is to come.

Trying to shrink the black race
Will do you no good,
Because people of color are worldwide,
And people without color are shrinking —
Very rapidly.

You have dug many holes,
You have set many traps,
And you're falling
Into every last one of them.

You have created a race of people
Which are still people of color,
And you call them bi-racial,
But they're still people of color.
One who has no color will eventually
Find someone of color, male or female,
And return to that from which it came.
So each and every day,
It will become very clear to you
That you cannot stop the race from shrinking.

Eliminating the evil
From the shrinking race
Will allow us to come together
As Brothers and Sisters,
As it was written.

We will become as one
And live in peace and harmony.
No longer will we have to worry about
The human race shrinking,

Looking Over My Life

I thought my life would be a giant cobweb
With me caught up in it,
Wondering when the big spider was coming,
And what I would do when it came for me.
This is how life seemed to me.
Going a hundred miles an hour
And going nowhere.

So I said to myself,
"What can I do to make my life better?
Look at all the negative things,
Or look at all the positive things?"
I chose positive.
There's no room in my mind
For negative things.
I'm going to succeed,
No matter what it takes.

There were a lot of stumbling blocks
Out there that I hurdled over,
A lot of negative talk that
I refused to listen to.
This is my life,
And I'm going to do
The best I can for it.

Whatever I do,
However I succeed,
I will make a way for anybody else
Who chooses to follow.

I will share whatever I have,
Knowledge and finance.
Sad days come —
A lot of them —
And sad days go.
But I never continue to think
That sadness lasts forever
Because I know that just around the corner
A cloudy day will clear
And the sun will come out again.

You know,
Just to hate someone
Is no longer in my heart and mind.
Sometimes I wonder where did it go,
Because I had a lot of hate
In my heart and in my mind
For anyone who did me wrong.
Now it's hard for me
To hate anyone or dislike them.

I feel something
And I don't know what it is.
Sometimes I sit alone
And want to cry,
But not a tear falls.

Sometimes I think that if I had one wish,
I would wish that everybody on this earth
Were truly satisfied with themselves,
Because when you are,
Nothing else matters.
For all which surrounds us,
I pray to God that greed never becomes us,
Like it has so many others.

I look at the times that I was working
And tried to do all that I could
To help my employer,
Knowing that he did all that he could
To fire me.
But that wasn't going to happen
Because I studied his ways,
I studied his moves,
Just like a checkerboard.
But I was the one doing all the jumping.

I've seen so many things in my life
That have made me happy —
That have made me sad.
But life goes on — with you or without you —
And I say, never hang your head down,
No matter how bad it may be
Or how bad things may get.
Always stand proud for whatever you have,
Or whatever you don't have.
As long as you're happy with yourself,
Everything is going to be all right.

Never let material stuff
Stand in the way of helping someone.
Don't ever think that someone you are helping
Is using you.
If he or she thinks that,
They're only using themselves.
So never let anyone deter you
From helping someone.

I've seen people who have done so much bad,
Yet I've seen people who have done so much good.
And that's what I prefer to look at —
The good side, not the bad side.

I have no anger in my heart for my employer.
I have no anger in my heart for my enemy.

Looking over my life,
I've seen so much good.
I've seen people reaching out
To help me in every way possible.
Now I must return this and try
To help as many as I possibly can.
I am willing to sacrifice whatever I have
That is mine, materialistically,
Or my own life,
To do whatever I can to help my fellowman,
My Sisters and Brothers.

Looking over my life and the way I used to think,
I thank God I don't think that way any more.
Looking over my life.